NASHVILLE PUBLIC LIBRARY

FOUNDATION

*This book given
to the Nashville Public Library
through the generosity of the*
**Dollar General
Literacy Foundation**

NPLF.ORG

PowerKiDS
Readers

Happy Holidays!

Thanksgiving

Josie Keogh

PowerKiDS
press.

New York

Published in 2013 by The Rosen Publishing Group, Inc.
29 East 21st Street, New York, NY 10010

First Edition

Editor: Amelie von Zumbusch
Book Design: Andrew Povolny

Photo Credits: Cover JGI/Jamie Grill/Blend Images/Getty Images; p. 5 Taylor Hill/FilmMagic/Getty Images; p. 7 Ryan McVay/Photodisc/Thinkstock; p. 9 Ariel Skelley/Blend Images/Getty Images; p. 11 Stockbyte/Getty Images; p. 13 Alexandra Grablewski/Lifesize/Thinkstock; p. 15 Sean Justice/The Image Bank/Getty Images; p. 17 Creatas Images/Creatas/Thinkstock; p. 19 iStockphoto/Thinkstock; p. 21 Jupiterimages/LiquidLibrary/Thinkstock; p. 23 SuperStock/Getty Images.

Library of Congress Cataloging-in-Publication Data

Keogh, Josie.
 Thanksgiving / by Josie Keogh. — 1st ed.
   p. cm. — (Powerkids readers: happy holidays!)
 Includes index.
 ISBN 978-1-4488-9624-0 (library binding) — ISBN 978-1-4488-9704-9 (pbk.) —
 ISBN 978-1-4488-9705-6 (6-pack)
 1. Thanksgiving Day—Juvenile literature. I. Title.
 GT4975.K46 2013
 394.2649—dc23
                            2012020043

Manufactured in the United States of America

CPSIA Compliance Information: Batch #W13PK3: For Further Information contact Rosen Publishing, New York, New York at 1-800-237-9932

Contents

It is Thanksgiving!

5

There is a big meal.

7

It is fun to cook.

8

Apple is the top **pie**.

Cranberries grow in bogs.

12

13

Peas come from pods.

15

Corn grows as ears.

Male **turkeys** are toms.

The first Thanksgiving
was in 1621.

20

21

It lasted for three days!

WORDS TO KNOW

cranberries

pies

turkey

INDEX

WEBSITES

Due to the changing nature of Internet links, PowerKids Press has developed an online list of websites related to the subject of this book. This site is updated regularly. Please use this link to access the list:
www.powerkidslinks.com/pkrhh/thanks/